The Life Cycle of a

Frog

by Lisa Trumbauer

Consulting Editor: Gail Saunders-Smith, Ph.D.

Consultant: Ronald L. Rutowski, Professor,
Department of Biology, Arizona State University

Pebble Books

an imprint of Capstone Press
Mankato, Minnesota

Pebble Books are published by Capstone Press
151 Good Counsel Drive, P.O. Box 669, Mankato, Minnesota 56002
http://www.capstone-press.com

1 2 3 4 5 6 07 06 05 04 03 02

Library of Congress Cataloging-in-Publication Data
Trumbauer, Lisa, 1963–
    The life cycle of a frog/by Lisa Trumbauer.
    p. cm—(Life cycles)
    Includes bibliographical references (p. 23) and index.
    Summary: Simple text and photographs present the life cycle of frogs, from egg
to tadpole to full-grown frog.
    ISBN 0-7368-1185-0
    1. Frogs—Life cycles—Juvenile literature. [1. Frogs. 2. Tadpoles.] I. Title. II.
Life cycles (Mankato, Minn.)
QL668.E2 T78 2002
597.8′9—dc21   2001003111

Note to Parents and Teachers

The Life Cycles series supports national science standards related to life science. This book describes and illustrates the life cycle of a wood frog. The photographs support early readers in understanding the text. The repetition of words and phrases helps early readers learn new words. This book also introduces early readers to subject-specific vocabulary words, which are defined in the Words to Know section. Early readers may need assistance to read some words and to use the Table of Contents, Words to Know, Read More, Internet Sites, and Index/Word List sections of the book.

Table of Contents

Photographs in this book show the life cycle of a wood frog.

eggs

4

A frog begins life
as an egg in a pond.
It is one of thousands
of eggs in a spawn.

two weeks

A tadpole hatches
underwater after
one to three weeks.

three weeks

A long tail helps the tadpole swim.
The tadpole has gills to breathe underwater.

four weeks

Lungs begin to grow after four weeks. The tadpole breathes above water.

eight weeks

The tadpole grows legs.
Its tail gets shorter
and disappears.

12 weeks

The tadpole becomes
a frog after 12 weeks.
The frog climbs out
of the pond.

adult

Some frogs can
live up to 10 years.

A female frog lays
a spawn of eggs
in a pond. A male
frog fertilizes the spawn.

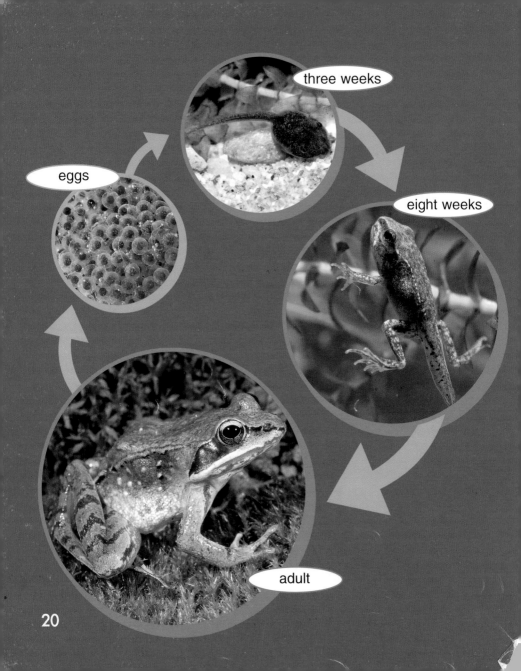

three weeks

eggs

eight weeks

adult

The eggs are the start of a new life cycle.

Words to Know

adult—an animal that is able to mate; most frogs continue to grow larger after becoming adults.

disappear—to go out of sight; a tadpole's tail disappears as it grows into a frog.

fertilize—to begin reproduction in an egg; male frogs fertilize eggs laid by female frogs.

gill—a body part on the side of a tadpole that helps it get oxygen underwater; a tadpole's gills start to close after four weeks.

hatch—to break out of an egg; tadpoles hatched from the same spawn stay close to the spawn for about two weeks.

life cycle—the stages in the life of an animal; the life cycle includes being born, growing up, having young, and dying.

spawn—the mass of eggs produced by female amphibians; eggs in a spawn are protected by jelly; spawns have from 2,000 to 3,000 eggs.

Read More

Kottke, Jan. *From Tadpole to Frog.* How Things Grow. New York: Children's Press, 2000.

Schaefer, Lola M. *Frogs: Leaping Amphibians.* The Wild World of Animals. Mankato, Minn.: Bridgestone Books, 2001.

Zoehfeld, Kathleen Weidner. *Tadpole to Frog.* Scholastic Science Readers. New York: Scholastic, 2001.

Internet Sites

Exploratorium
http://www.exploratorium.edu/frogs

Frogland
http://allaboutfrogs.org/froglnd.shtml

Something Froggy
http://www.fi.edu/fellows/fellow9/jun99

(Index/Word List

Word Count: 115
Early-Intervention Level: 14

Editorial Credits

Sarah Lynn Schuette, editor; Jennifer Schonborn, production designer and interior
   illustrator; Kia Bielke, cover designer; Kimberly Danger and Mary Englar,
   photo researchers

Photo Credits

Dwight R. Kuhn, cover, 1, 6, 8, 10, 12, 14, 16, 18, 20 (top, right, bottom)
Visuals Unlimited/Nathan Cohen, 4, 20 (left)